Decoding Direct Selling

Ritu Singh

BLUEROSE PUBLISHERS
India | U.K.

Copyright © Ritu Singh 2025

All rights reserved by author. No part of this publication may be reproduced, stored in a retrieval system or transmitted in any form or by any means, electronic, mechanical, photocopying, recording or otherwise, without the prior permission of the author. Although every precaution has been taken to verify the accuracy of the information contained herein, the publisher assumes no responsibility for any errors or omissions. No liability is assumed for damages that may result from the use of information contained within.

BlueRose Publishers takes no responsibility for any damages, losses, or liabilities that may arise from the use or misuse of the information, products, or services provided in this publication.

For permissions requests or inquiries regarding this publication, please contact:

BLUEROSE PUBLISHERS
www.BlueRoseONE.com
info@bluerosepublishers.com
+91 8882 898 898
+4407342408967

ISBN: 978-93-6783-982-9

First Edition: January 2025

About the author

Embark on a journey through the life of a true visionary, a versatile leader whose career spans over 34 years of inspiring excellence across diverse industries. From hospitality and travel to the dynamic world of direct selling, this book is a treasure trove of wisdom, drawn from decades of hands-on experience in nurturing, coaching, and empowering people.

The author's journey in direct selling started in 1996, marking the start of a transformative path in the direct selling industry. With unparalleled expertise and insights, working with top companies, shaping success stories and building resilient teams across India and beyond.

This book is not just a reflection of the past but a practical guide for anyone aspiring to lead, grow, and excel in an ever-evolving professional landscape. Discover strategies, stories, and secrets to thrive in direct selling and beyond, crafted by someone who has lived and breathed these industries for decades.

A must-read for aspiring leaders, industry professionals, and anyone seeking inspiration from a life well-lived and lessons well-learned.

Ritu Singh

Acknowledgement

I would like to thank my daughter Ratika Singh who motivated me to write this book. She's always been there with her extended support.

I would also like to thank my family and friends for their encouragement.

Contents

Let's Get Started 1
Introduction 4
Success in network marketing 6
What is Network Marketing? 8
Understanding how the business works 12
Dreams 14
Training and Support System 18
Product Knowledge and Selling 21
Prospecting 22
Contact List / Memory Jogger 24
Inviting People 25
Call Reluctance 27
Overcoming Objections 30
Closing 35
Think Big and Believe you can Succeed! 37
Retention 41
Selling 43
How do I identify leaders ? 53
Sorting for Potential leaders 58

Let's Get Started

A few tips to remember before starting this business.

- Stop overthinking about results, thinking to a certain extent is good but at times overthinking causes stress and self-doubt.
- Filling our minds with fear, worry, negative thoughts keep us away from being our best.
- Focusing on things within our control such as our attitude, aspiration, dreams, spending quality time by reading books, listening to podcasts and watching motivational videos.
- Taking small steps, action is the most important step towards success. Great ideas are useless if not executed appropriately.

Self-Belief and Self Realization

Before starting this business, we need to believe in ourselves, for that we need to know, why I want to do this business, who we are and where do I want to go with this business.

Now the question you need to ask yourself is what is required of me to start this business, and do I have the ability to do so?

To gear up to the questions above you need to do SWOT Analysis to identify your strengths, weaknesses, opportunities, and threats.

Now write down:

Your strengths

What do you do better than others? What unique capabilities do you have?

What do others perceive as your strength?

Your Weakness

What are your weaknesses? What steps can you take to improve?

Whatdo other people do better than you?

What do others perceive as your weakness?

What Opportunities do you have?

Available opportunities at present.

What conditions may positively impact you.?

Threats

What conditions negatively impact you?

What are others doing that may impact you?

What impact does your weakness have on the threats to you?

Do you have a solid financial support?

Now once we are clear on SWOT Analysis of ourselves, we can start the self-realization factor, which is believing in yourself.

Why do we need to believe in ourselves?

- So that we are in control of our thoughts and feelings
- So that we trust ourselves and set realistic goals and expectations, communicate assertively and handle criticism.
- So that we are more focused and our productivity increases.
- So that it helps you develop mental strength, sustains your vision and strengths your willpower.
- Building confidence to overcome any obstacles attracts people towards you.
- It gives a sense of comfort, purpose, and connections to others especially during challenging times.
- It's a skill that you can grow with time, it's not an emotion, it's a belief in one's abilities and qualities that come from experience.

Believing in yourself is very important as it gives you a feeling that you're in control of your life, you start to believe in yourself more and it boosts your confidence. Self-believe has the power to either limit you from reaching your full potential or propel you to do great things.

Confidence initiates you to act, it also encourages you to take bigger risks which result in bigger rewards.

Self-confidence helps you overcome any obstacles and face any challenges that come in your way. The only way to improve your self-confidence is to start trusting yourself.

Self-trust is one's relationship with oneself. It's how much you trust yourself and your inner voice. When we are confident, we make better decisions. We are not bothered by what others are saying about our abilities and with a positive attitude we can achieve success.

Introduction

In the network marketing business, we meet many people from different regions, cultures and dialects. I am sharing with you my experience of over 30 years and knowledge that I have gained in my journey of network marketing. This business is all about understanding people, empathizing with them during their ups & downs with a growth mindset, yes you need to be open to learning at all times.

Your biggest challenge is not the product or opportunity but it's the people. Yes people – understanding, managing, motivating, mentoring & teaching them along with leading them. The more you understand about the nitty gritties or psychology of this business, the better you would be at building yourself, your team, network and business.

Since this business is a peoples business the first thing we need to understand is what is a mindset, as every individual in your network would have a different mindset which means mental attitude that determines how you will perceive a situation or interpret or respond to situations. In summary what's your attitude towards life involving beliefs, feelings, values and dispositions to act in certain ways.

We need to have a growth mind set to be successful in this business, meaning we need to believe that our abilities can be developed through hard work, learning new strategies and open for feedback when we are stuck. People may start with different temperaments, but experience, training and personal efforts can take them forward.

Your mindset is the key to your success, be aware of your feelings, what thoughts are causing these feelings and get geared into positiveness, then take action.

You can change your mindset and attitude by practicing gratitude /mindfulness, reading books, fostering positive relationships, visualizing success, setting goals and actioning them.

Another important factor we need to look into is our habit. Just like money multiplies through compound interest, the effects of your habits with small steps keep adding up to enormous results. The first thing of building a good habit is discipline, that means whatever goals you have set for yourself can be achieved when you plan it with a process and design small steps within the process so there are no gaps.

This book is designed in such a way that you would be able to identify the roadblocks that derail you, help you come back on track through techniques that will empower you and your network to be successful.

Success in network marketing

When we realize our fears and practice to overcome them, we can stop sabotaging our hopes and dreams.

People buy in to the business on an emotional high and buy out on an emotional low. Like every aspect of life, people's emotions play a huge part in their business.

To succeed in the network marketing business, you must learn how to manage your emotions. The key to success and longevity is your ability to recruit and retain good people.

Since it's a people's business and people are emotional beings, you need to understand them individually so that you can manage and motivate them. It's not an easy job to build a strong team. You will have to learn to climb the ladder of success.

At this stage, you need to be a good listener because no one cares about how much you know until they know how much you care. In other words, how much you care about people counts more than how much you know about the product and opportunity.

30% to 50% of success depends on choosing the "WHAT", that is choosing what you know about the product and opportunity whereas 70% to 90% depends on choosing the "WHO" that is who you recruit and give your time to.

Leaders who invest their time and efforts in people are the ones who build large productive teams.

"This book will help everyone, from a prospect who wants to learn more about this business, to a new recruit who recently signed up, to a person struggling to get results to a leader who's been in this business for a long time and has built a successful team. "

To attain success in the network marketing business, one needs to keep recruiting and retaining people.

The biggest challenge is managing people and therefore, it's important to learn this task properly. As mentioned above, the first step is to be a good listener. Dealing with emotions is an on-going process.

You should never lose focus on your goal or the purpose of your involvement in this profession.

There can be different reasons as to why people may join this business, such as:

- To help others by sharing products and opportunities.
- To grow as a person and support others in their personal growth.
- To earn extra income while working flexible hours.
- To get recognition, travel abroad, and meet new people.
- To control destiny by owning a potentially high-profit home based business.

No matter what your purpose is, it can be accomplished via the network marketing business as it is a growing industry and has a bright future.

This book will guide you on how to start a business, what challenges you may face and how you can overcome them and become successful.

> *"You don't build a business; you build people and then people build the business"*
>
> *– Zig Ziglar*

What is Network Marketing?

Networking marketing business is the fastest way of moving products to the customer without middlemen or advertisement support. It's all about empowering an average person to have a lifelong source of income.

Network marketing is not a job but a fantastic business opportunity which has a proven success record, you are your own boss, you can plan your business as per your convenience and work with anyone of your choice wherever and whenever you want based on what you want to earn.

It's a flexible business which could be easily adapted to suit your lifestyle without hindering your other activities. It works on the system of exponential growth of business, which is achieved through compounding, leveraging time, energy, efforts, talents of others for yourself and of yourself for others.

"I'd prefer to work towards getting 1% effort from 100 people rather than 100% of my own effort."

Why Networking Marketing?

Network marketing has opportunities which can be incredibly rewarding on many levels and challenging like many mainstream businesses.

You need to work hard and smartly, as success is about being smarter and doing things differently, in a way we would have done not them previously. This approach not only allows you to work more effectively but also gives you the opportunity to associate with successful individuals who embrace this mindset and have already achieved success.

Leveraging and duplicating is simply the ability to leverage your time and to duplicate your efforts. In traditional business your income is largely governed by the number of hours you put in a week or in a month.

As your network grows, the time collectively invested within the network is dramatically increased and your efforts are greatly multiplied.

You start getting passive income which means that with time you don't have to physically do the work, but you can still maintain the income. Given the choice, most people would prefer passive income over active income.

One attractive feature of building this business is the low investment required to get started. If a person gets into a successfully developed network marketing organization, the return on such investment would be significant. The ongoing operating costs required in majority of these businesses is generally very low when compared to traditional businesses producing similar turnover. Cost often revolves around accessing educational and motivational materials, acquiring business building tools and attending seminars. There are some incidental costs as well such as mobile bills, fuel and other small office operating costs.

One major advantage of being involved in network marketing is the opportunity to establish it part time along with your current occupation or traditional business.

Some people fear taking the risk of giving up their secure jobs and regular income to an unknown business of networking. Therefore, it's recommended to work part time until you are comfortable enough and are earning a sufficient amount. Later on, you can switch full time to networking if you like it.

An important thing you need to know is that thousands of people have made money from network marketing but there are some who have not made any because they were not aligned to the system. They were not teachable, did not listen, nor were active enough, to give sufficient time to work and most importantly did not treat this as a real business. The seriousness was not there.

You need to find the right network marketing business for yourself.

Please remember "if you don't work in your business the business won't work for you."

Network marketing has become a victim of too many misconceptions. Today companies have to adhere to strict code of conduct, ethics, product standards, quality, and company details on their website.

Network marketing and its acceptance are growing with an increasing number of companies operating globally. Their business models, products, culture, bonus/incentives, and remuneration can vary considerably. It's important to understand this variation rather than thinking of them as the same.

Remember the aim is to build a successful network for a long-term passive income.

Before taking the decision to join in, ensure credibility, stability of the company and its business model. Now that you have chosen the company, the next question that comes to the mind is 'Can I do it?,' 'Am I the right type of person for this business?" The answer is 'Yes you can' and 'Yes you are.' Every person's journey is different in network marketing. Some who join come with past experience, skills & confidence that makes it easier for them. While others come with little experience and confidence, which may create some challenges. What we need to understand is that both categories of people would be successful, but the time to achieve success would differ.

Many fail, but many succeed in a big way.

There are many people who have failed in network marketing as there are many who have failed in weight loss, learning a musical instrument, a new language but that doesn't mean that they can never lose weight or learn a musical instrument or a new language. The reality is that there will always be a percentage of failures in most endeavors but as long as there's a percentage of success, it's an enough proof that you can succeed.

Some challenges you may face when starting this business:

- Coming out of your comfort zone.
- Family and friends being negative on why you are doing this.
- Getting frustrated, as to why it's taking so long to achieve success.
- Not always achieving your targets.
- Doing additional work on top of what you are already doing.

Your attitude to overcome these challenges will determine your success. Secondly, how committed you are for this business to achieve success.

You may not like everything about this business.

Getting started is not always going to be as per your convenience and it might mean sacrificing some things like your social life, your time with family and friends etc. but these are only short adjustments till your business is established.

We need to realize that there will be certain things which we don't like doing or don't agree with but at that time we need to be focused and positive.

Understanding how the business works

Like every industry, network marketing has its own terminology (jargons). It's important for you to understand them. Almost all terminologies within the network marketing business are similar across globally. Terms such as down- line, sponsoring, line of sponsorship, groups, consultant, associate, and distributors are commonly used to describe a structure within a network.

Terms such as diamond, emerald, platinum, director, manager and senior manager may be used to indicate levels of achievement or positions within a hierarchy. There might be other specific terms used in other companies.

As a business owner it's important for you to familiarize yourself with your line of sponsorship, build a rapport/relationship particularly with those above you. The people above you (line of sponsorships) would provide you with unlimited knowledge, skills and information based on their experience because they have been involved in this business longer than you. In many cases they would become your mentors and would be there to support you in building a successful business.

Remember to understand the compensation plan completely as in some companies, the way you structure your business in terms of people in your network can have a significant impact on your remuneration and profitability. In other cases, particular products may be more profitable to promote and used than others.

Recognition and rewards are an important aspect of this business. This alone can be a driving force to achieve success. Many networking companies also have non- cash incentives such as seminars, travel, cars, travel funds, housing funds and holidays for achievement. Many well-established network marketing companies have written rules of conduct or guidelines that set out the roles and responsibilities of not only the company but of the networker / independent business owner / independent consultant also.

As an independent business entrepreneur or networker, you should familiarize yourself with them and always adhere to them. You should become an advocate for this business. Be ethical in all your work and display an unimpeachable behavior. You need to make it clear to your downlines that they need to be ethical and you except same standards from them.

Dreams

Dreams are the foundation of success. Most of our accomplishments, whether personal or professional, start with a dream. Whether big or small they motivate us to take an action. We are all born to dream and have the ability to achieve them but at times with age as we get older many of us lose sight of them. Network marketing potentially opens a door to achieve them. Take time to be clear on what your goals and aspirations in life are and once you know them, your chances of achieving them are greatly increased.

The biggest problem with people is that they are always thinking about what they don't want (within their subconsciousness), and then they wonder why it shows up in their thoughts over and over again. We should hold on to the thoughts of what we want, make it absolutely clear in our minds and from that we start to understand the law of attraction. You not only become what you think about the most, but you also attract it as well. It takes courage to feel the fear and the risk.

> *"If you are interested, you will do what is convenient, if you are committed, you will do whatever it takes"*
>
> *– John Assaraf*

What are your dreams?

- Big House
- Luxury Car
- Foreign Trips
- Higher Education for children
- Children Marriage
- Security
- Recognition

- Better lifestyle
- Financial Freedom
- Flexible Hours
- Personal Growth
- Socializing / Fun

First break down your dreams into short term, medium term and long-term. Then visualize them by being specific.

For example, you can dream of having a luxury car.

What type of car – BMW

The model number – BMW X3

The color – White

Date – When you will buy the car

Draw the car or put a picture of the car in a place where you can see it regularly. It could be on the fridge, your almirah, bathroom, on the mirror or on your bedroom wall. Successful people surround themselves with their dreams, immerse themselves in it and already imagine that they are living it.

Building on your dreams is also important, when you achieve them don't stop there, but go on and achieve the next one. Review your dreams daily. Your networking business is simply the vehicle you are using to achieve them, and your dreams are the fuel that drives it.

In your path to success, you will find people who will try to hinder your dreams.

They will say 'be realistic, stop dreaming' or worse make fun of you, laugh at you and put you down. Don't allow these people to affect you in any way towards your journey to achieve your goals.

Now in order to put your dreams into reality we need to do goal setting.

Your dreams and goals will not change but the journey on how you reach your destination might change. At times when we are travelling to a destination on a particular route, we might face obstacles and may need to change the route to reach our final destination.

When setting goals, we identify people within our network who can contribute to your success. However, there are times when some may drop out for various reasons. In such cases, we need to find others in our network who can step in and help you achieve your goals.

Goals are important because they give us a sense of direction. How can you reach your destination if it's not defined?

Destination Determines Direction.

Goals are dreams that have a deadline, a defined path, and a concrete plan of action. Dreams become goals only when they are supported by Direction, Dedication, Determination, Discipline and Deadline. They are result oriented and not activity oriented. We should know that there are no results without activity, however not all activities give results.

Hence, we should choose our activities carefully and prioritize them.

As per survey's done, 97% of the people don't do goal setting and less than 3%do it.

Reasons why people don't do goal setting:

- **Pessimistic Attitude**-These people are negative; they are looking for excuses instead of possibilities.
- **Fear of Failure** - People are afraid of failing; they think if they don't set goals they won't fail.
- **Fear of Rejection**- Worrying about what others might think if one is not successful in doing something. Our low self-esteem makes us believe that other people's opinion is more important than ours. This shows lack of confidence.
- **Procrastination-** Lack of ambition
- **Lack of knowledge** - About setting goals and not clear on how important it is.

Our goals should be aligned with our needs and wants. Therefore, we need to have **SMART GOALS**.

S – Specific (It should be planned and pre-conceived)

M – Measurable (It should be precise)

A – Achievable (We should confirm that they are reachable)

R – Realistic (Flexible enough to suit our convenience so that we can reschedule it)

T – Time Bound (It should be achieved within a certain time frame)

Goal setting should be bifurcated into three broad categories:

Short term

Mid term

Long term

Please ensure that your goals are realistic and achievable. They should be slightly out of reach but not out of sight. Focus should be clear while setting goals. The action plan should clarify what to do, when to do and who will do it, by when.

Training and Support System

One of the best benefits of network marketing is that even though you are in business for yourself you are never in business by yourself.

Network marketing provides a great training and support mechanism which unfortunately is often not utilized enough. A major benefit of this business is to get support from experienced resources who have been in it for many years and have been successful. A mistake which many new people coming into this business make is that they think they know how to run this business as they are from sales business background and are already motivated.

You should be a part of the support system; it will help you to learn and grow your business, you can say that support systems are the universe of network marketing. To be successful you need to be a part of the support system and encourage your network for the same.

The training and support systems provide you with knowledge that gives you the skills necessary to build a successful network and increase your income. You need to find a coach within your network who can assist you in building your business. A coach would be someone above you in your direct line, or someone who has vested interest in your success.

Find someone who is genuinely working with the system, and with whom you have a rapport become a good student and be open to learning. If you don't have enough knowledge, you would not react because of lack of confidence, but if you acted with lack of knowledge, it would give you less favorable results which would further lead to disappointment. If you are open-minded, teachable, and bright, then the knowledge gained will give you confidence and success.

Duplication:

The key to develop a successful network marketing business is to be someone that others in your team can duplicate. Building a strong network means building a system of people who themselves are developing their own business and are following the same proven system.

Encourage your team to use the sales tools provided by the company.

Develop Yourself:

You can only develop yourself if you move out of your comfort zone. This can be challenging but it can mean the difference between success and failure. It also means that you are growing personally.

One big thing that holds people back from achieving success is FEAR. Fear can be in many forms – of people, failure, success, rejection or change. You will overcome this only when you take an action and see the reality, that's when the perception of fear will be diminished.

Motivation is simply the fuel to drive your business forward. The degree of motivation in network marketing is the real asset so get yourself motivated and motivate your network regularly.

You need to dress up professionally as you need to make an impression that you're a professional businessperson who displays confidence.

Network Building:

Fundamentally networking is all about building a business with other people who want the opportunity to improve their lifestyles financially and achieve their dreams.

An important thing you must remember while building your network is that you should know the dreams of the people in your team and support them to achieve it. This business is about people, if you build the people, the sale of the product will come by default.

Develop your people's skills as its important to understand human behavior and those we are endeavoring to work and interact with. Investing your energy, time and money in this area will pay off at every level, since your team would be having people from different cultures, various backgrounds, occupations and personality types. Therefore, it's important that you learn about these different personalities. Understanding them would help you to identify your strengths and weaknesses so that you can work on improving them. It will also help you overall in how to interact with other people. Now look at yourself as a leader that you want to be.

Success in network marketing is fundamentally a team effort. By motivating team's spirit and getting everybody involved, it would create enthusiasm and excitement which will lead to achievement of your goals.

Your success can only be achieved when you help others in your network to achieve their goals and dreams. If you find people in your team who suffer from lack of confidence or low self - esteem, you must do your best to empower them with your genuine belief by assuring that you will stand with them and make it happen. Telling someone that you believe in them, that they can do it is never a waste of time. Leading by example sends out a message that you're serious and it builds confidence within your team . Your team will become inspired, and this will result in rapid growth.

Your role is to lead and empower those in your team and not to boss them. As a mentor, you advise and counsel your team but leave it up to them to make the final decision on what they should do.

Product Knowledge and Selling

As a business owner, in networking some products or services need to be sold if you want to make profit. It's very important that you have a good knowledge and understanding of the products or services which the business supplies. You must know the features and benefits of your products and the advantages they have over the competition. You must also believe in the quality and value of your product if you are to inspire others to join you in your network and sell them to customers. You can educate yourself with product knowledge through company's product literature, videos, product trainings and workshops / seminars.

You need to be a 100% user of your own products. Remember this business is all about duplication. So, if you are not using your own products, the people in your network will see this as a message that you don't believe in what you're doing.

Every business involves the need to sell, and the level of selling varies, it is not just about selling products or services but in many cases it's also about selling yourself (your confidence of what you're proposing) and your business. People who are building their network marketing business will sometimes raise objections like I don't like to sell, or I don't see myself as a salesperson. The type and amount of selling required will vary depending on the network marketing company you are associated with.

In most cases you will need to sell products and business concepts whereas in some the business is driven by business owners selling products to retail customers and in some you need to build volume through your network combined with a small amount of retail selling.

Generating retail profit from selling products is a great resource for covering expenses.

Prospecting

Prospecting is identifying people potentially interested in whatever your business may be offering. We can also say that prospecting is a process of reaching out to potential customers in hope of finding new business. It is often the first part of the sales process that comes before follow-up, communication and sales activity.

It is the lifeblood of network marketing business and key to success in sales.

No matter how good you're doing, you must always do prospecting and encourage everyone in your network to do prospecting.

We need to do prospecting because no matter what happens there will always be a certain percentage of people in your network base who will leave you, and eventually your network will become stagnant and then nonexistent. Therefore, it's of utmost importance that you keep prospecting.

Your recruitment must be greater than your outflow. In other words, we need to fill up our network bucket and continue to grow. If we don't recruit our bucket will become empty (the bucket has holes, or we can say that the bucket is leaking)

Two Reasons why we do prospecting:

- Increase sales and replace customers that would be lost overtime.
- Find people that have been looking for money, authority and have a desire to buy.

In networking new customers / distributors come into the top and leave through a hole at the bottom of the bucket because they are not satisfied with our service therefore it's important to take care of our existing customers / distributors as the cost of acquiring a new customer is higher than keeping an existing customer, this is why service and follow up after the sale is very important.

Some methods of prospecting:

- E-prospecting on web (websites/blogs)
- Social Media (Facebook, Instagram)
- Telemarketing
- Cold Calling
- Advertisement
- Exhibitions
- Trade Shows
- Referrals
- Kitty Parties
- Your personal kit

Contact List / Memory Jogger

The first step in building your network marketing business is to make a list of all the people you know. Simply write down the names of everyone you have ever known or met. They may be family, friends, work colleagues or people you know on a casual basis.

When making this list don't worry about who might or might not be interested. Don't pre-judge people, as you never know who would join your network. Pre-judging is assuming that a particular person won't be interested in the business opportunity for reasons such as they might be too busy, they are quite well to do, they would not be interested in selling etc. You should not judge people as it might lead to missing out on opportunities.

Remember to keep updating your list regularly by adding new names. This contact list is the selling foundation of your business.

For example.

Name	Contact No.	Profession	Address	Email	Birthday	Remarks
Neha	X99955672	Teacher	Noida	neha234@xmail.com	30th June	-

Inviting People

Once your contact list is done, let's start inviting people to look at what you're doing with the view that it might be something that they would also be interested in. Your coach or mentor can assist you with your first few calls of invitation.

Some important points to remember before making the call:
- The introduction should be short.
- Ask if it's a convenient time to talk.
- Be enthusiastic and excited when you're talking.

Some inviting phrases:
- Would you like to participate in a business project that has the potential to be a bigger than a well - known organization.
- Do you ever look at business ideas.
- Have you ever considered other ways of earning besides your regular 9 to 5 job.

Dos of inviting:
- Be excited and enthusiastic.
- Share with them that you're expanding your business.
- Create a sense of urgency and curiosity.
- Invite at least three times more people than your seating capacity at home or otherwise.
- Be positive, relax and enjoy.
- Take confirmed commitment on the appointment.
- Encourage them to bring their spouse.
- Make it clear that there is no obligation, only sharing new information for their benefits.

Don'ts of inviting:

- Don't tell them too much on the phone.
- There should be no hesitation in calling people.
- You should not be nervous.
- Don't be pushy or pressurize anyone.
- Don't approach people covertly. They should know that you are talking about an opportunity to benefit them.

The first few invitation calls, which is done with your upline, mentor is called three way calling. It is a process in which your upline/coach teaches you how to invite. This three-way calling converts a possible negative response to a positive action of readiness to attend.

The only reason why we don't give out too much information on the phone is because they cannot clearly see the opportunity to its fullest. They will make up their minds based on the small amount of information you have said rather than the whole picture.

Therefore, it's important to keep people curious rather than trying to get into the details. Understand that this is a normal business practice used extensively in both network marketing and traditional businesses.

The best practice is to explain your product, service and business opportunity face to face in a professional environment. It would be great if you're presenting to both husband & wife together so that instant decision can be made, and any objections can be handled simultaneously.

Call Reluctance

Many people are reluctant to call. It's a fear which holds one back, but procrastination is an indication that a problem is developing. You must have self- belief and practice in front of the mirror before making invite calls.

Call reluctance is an emotion which we need to overcome with confidence, this can only be done by picking up the phone and inviting a prospect.

WHO IS A PROSPECT?

A prospect is someone who must have these two qualities to become a distributor/consultant/associate or whatever terminology your company has.

- DESIRE: The desire to earn extra money. A big mistake many people make is by confusing needs with desires. There are people who need extra money but have no desire/hunger to earn it.

  An unemployed person may need extra money but may not have the desire to go out and earn it. They may be satisfied with what they have. Therefore, it's important at this stage that we identify our prospect.

- TIME: Everyone has 24 hours in their lives, and we are looking for someone who is willing to set aside time to work with you in building the network. We need prospects who can give 8 to 12 hours a week with commitment. There might be some who would say they will give 4 to 6 hours a week and that is also acceptable.

Since we are clear on qualities required to become a good networker, now all we need to do is ask these questions in the initial stage.

- Do you want to earn some extra money?
- Are you willing to set aside 8 to 12 hours a week?

With these questions we can get down to business by giving the person the desire for an opportunity.

After inviting the prospect for a meeting, you will present to them the product and the business opportunity in detail. This can be done on a one-to-one basis or in a small group at someone's home. The preferred method might vary from company to company and in many cases, you would be involved in seminars with a guest speaker doing the presentation.

Initially your upline/coach would do a few meetings for you and with you but only later you will have to duplicate what you have learned.

If you are presenting the opportunity to a couple, it's important to make sure that both of them are present. You will often notice that if you show the presentation to one of them and they get excited then they will try to explain it to their partner when you are not there. They would not be able to explain it properly and answer the questions. The result would be that they would not join.

When your prospective client decides to join your network after seeing your presentation it's important that you get to know them and build a good rapport with them.

It's a people-driven business, so it's essential to take a genuine interest in building relationships with those in your network to create a successful business.

During your presentations you should sell the dream, not the business. People usually join on emotions of what they see they can get from the opportunity and not necessarily the opportunity itself. For many people your presentation provides the chance of achieving dreams or goals which they feel can't be achieved by what they are currently doing. Your goal should be to find out what their dreams are and then talk about how this network marketing business opportunity can help them achieve those dreams.

Presenting the opportunity is not about selling the business concept but it's about showing the prospect how this business vehicle can be used to fulfil their dreams. It is important to remember that this business is simply a vehicle, and the dream drives it, so without the fuel the vehicle cannot move.

Please don't get into too much detailing in your first presentation with the prospect and ensure that you book the next meeting before leaving the current one.

Overcoming Objections

Whenever you are presenting an idea in any context you will always be confronted with occasional objections. Objections are sometimes questions in disguise.

It's very rare that any sales presentation is taking place without objections. Handling an objection is an integral part of the selling process.

Objections are rejections and should not be taken personally. They are only questions asking for more information. Every objection is an opportunity to close. Whenever a prospect or any person makes an objection, they are saying we have doubts, and we are not satisfied.

Objections arise because of some of the following reasons:

- Need is not clear – Not interested.
- Monetary issues – It's too expensive.
- Satisfied with existing products.
- Not confident about you, the products and the compensation plan (lack of trust)
- Give me some time, I will get back to you!

These usually arise because of lack of communication, now this can mean incomplete information or lack of trust or misunderstanding.

Sometimes objections are questions in disguise for example in a case where your prospect says I am interested but I don't think I have the time – can you advise it that's okay. Here you need to find if it's a genuine objection and your prospect is saying no to the idea or whether it's a question in disguise and your prospect is saying yes if you have a positive answer. In a situation like this you should ask your prospect "If I can help you overcome that, would you be interested in getting started."

Without asking you will never know whether it's a genuine objection or a question in disguise which hinders your ability to make the presentation a success.

We need to learn how to overcome these. It's a skill you will build with time.

You need to guide people from overcoming objections to taking the first step, as those who are interested often express it through their body language or questions, rather than directly saying so. They are looking for you to lead them in getting started.

Understand that you are leading people not pushing them. They cannot be led if they don't want to be.

Challenges:
- Some of the challenges we all face in network marketing is coping with rejection. We should know how to handle rejections and not take them personally. Many have failed because they had difficulty in coming to terms with reality.
- Secondly people factor is another challenge, as your network would consist of people from different backgrounds, ages, nationalities and personalities. Many would bring with them their past experiences such as relationship issues, past failures and lack of confidence along with the day-to-day challenges which we all face.
- You must understand that you cannot please everyone, nor can you solve all their problems. The best you can do is try to be a friend and improve your people's skills.
- Thirdly there would be many people who would disappoint you when you are developing your network. For example, people who join your network might not stay on for long. There would be some with whom you have spent a lot of time and efforts, and they might decide to leave or not remain involved. Others who back out may even include those who you thought were going to be the key people, an integral part of your business structure in achieving your goals. There will be others who will simply not be

active as you would like them to be, and some would say one thing and do another.

- Fourthly, politics will inevitably grow as your network grows. Politics can arise within your own team, between your team and another, between leaders in the business, between the company and its support system or between the company and you (independent business owners). You need to understand that this aspect of your business is not negative, it's just a challenge of building a successful network.

- People's perception should not worry you in developing your network, as some perceptions would be positive and some negative. There would be many times when you are not able to achieve your goals so at that point of time you must remember never to give up.

- Positive attitude is one of the most important factors for success. Your attitude can literally determine your destiny. Successful people in all fields will tell you that the key to their success is their positive attitude. You really need to develop, or we can say learn how to control your attitude towards positivity.

As you are building your own network there would be many small and big problems like inventory being out of stock, delivery issues, wrong products being delivered or packaging issues. At this point of time, it's important that you don't lose your cool. You need to learn to be more proactive in solving problems instead of reacting to that situation.

You also need to be a problem solver rather than pilling on the problem and getting demotivated. You should develop the habit of reading positive books as it affects your attitude, and it would give you an amazing push towards building a successful network.

This business requires consistency and persistency. Consistency means step by step you are climbing the ladder of success. You also need to be persistent and maintain a never give up attitude.

Majority of successful people have had their own share of challenges and disappointments along the way but what got them to the top of the success ladder was their positive attitude combined with persistence.

As you build your network make a decision that you will persist no matter what.

Some tips for growing/developing your business:

- Always be keen to learn:

In life we must remember that no one knows everything. There is always room for every individual to learn more and more. Don't let yourself get too comfortable with the knowledge you have; you must have the hunger to learn more.

- Your words should mean a lot:

Keeping your word will build trust, confidence, dependability and reliability within your team. People will know that they can count on you, which is an important factor in developing a successful network.

- Listen to facts:

When you're building your network marketing business many people will give their opinions about what you do. This could be dangerous for a newcomer in the industry and since you do not know all the facts, you are more susceptible to being affected by mistaken opinions.

Because of being vulnerable to the opinions of others, most newcomers unfortunately decide not to continue.

- Keep your emotions balanced:

It's important to keep balance between your network marketing business, family, friends and others. Don't go overboard in just talking about your business that it becomes boring for others, and they start avoiding you.

- Criticism and other people's opinion:

Don't be bothered about what other people think about you. What's important is what you think. Secondly many people would start criticizing you, as you're ready to change and move from your comfort zone to an uncomfortable zone whereas they are not ready to change.

- Don't complain in front of your downlines:

If you have problems personally, financially or in your business, its best you talk to your upline. Negative environment is contagious as it demotivates and makes people feel bad about all aspects of life.

- Be Teachable:

This business of networking is all about duplication. You have to be a good student to learn and a good teacher to teach your network downlines. Knowledge leads to confidence and once you are confident, you act, and the action leads to results.

- Know your network thoroughly and be loyal to your organization:

Identifying key people in your network will help you better manage your time and allow you to provide quality advice to those who want it. Also, build your network structure in a profitable way and not just placing people one below the other in an abrupt manner.

Always promote leadership of your organization to your team, as it builds confidence in your team.

Closing

Every salesperson needs to close the sale after a good presentation or a good meeting. Closing is done only after you have identified the need of the prospect with a product and the right solution.

Many people are apprehensive of closing a sale or taking an order that they feel they are pushing. They say I will call you later, I will leave the catalogue/brochure with you, think about it or call me when you are comfortable.

This is self-destructive behavior. Let's not forget we are all paid for results not efforts. We don't get paid for prospecting, building relationships or making presentations. We get paid for closing the sale by getting the agreement signed, getting the order along with payment.

We must understand that closing is crucial because if we don't close it's a waste of time.

Closing Skills:

There are many closing techniques or skills, and everyone chooses their own techniques based on their own level of comfort.

Trial Close:

A trial close gives the person choice between buying or not buying. Trial close is more like taking an opinion. Examples of trial close are:

- What do you think about this product?
- Which flavor do your prefer or which color you prefer?
- When would you like it to be delivered, over the weekend or Monday?

The Silence Close:

In this closing, after you have done a good presentation and answered all the questions you maintain silence along with eye contact indicating to the prospect that now its his/her decision. Doing this puts pressure on the prospect to take a decision. The decision, whether positive or negative would depend upon the quality of your meeting/presentation. Remember in this technique of closing, don't break the silence and let the prospect/customer decide and talk.

At this point of time don't add anything.

Let the prospect talk first (break the silence) and then you can add on or answer his/her query.

Assumed Consent Close:

Assumed consent close means that the customer /prospect is answering all your questions and is aligned with you. Please ensure that during all your meetings or presentations you keep the registration forms/agreement forms on the table.

By doing this psychologically the prospect will know that the agreement form needs to be signed. Examples of some questions:

- Do you want to add your middle name?
- How do you spell your surname?
- How would you intake the payment?
- Do you want to add another address?

There are other closing techniques as well such as Conditional Close, Ben Franklin Close, Pointed Close etc. However, it all depends upon you which technique you're comfortable with looking at the situation.

Think Big and Believe you can Succeed!

Only a few people believe that they can succeed, their approach is positive, and they think they have reached the top and are successful. When you believe in yourself, the positive attitude generates power, skill and energy.

The "How to do it" always comes to the person who believes "He can do it." How to develop the power to belief:

Think about success and don't think of failure:

Whenever you face a difficult situation, think that I will win rather than thinking that I will probably lose.

When you compete with someone else, think that I am the best and not out classed.

When an opportunity appears, think that I can do it and never say I cannot.

Let your thoughts say that I will succeed, and you need to dominate/control your thinking process. Thinking success, conditions your mind to create plans that produce success. Thinking failure does the exact opposite.

- Remind yourself regularly that you are better than you think. Success is not mystical, and successful people are ordinary people who have developed belief in themselves that they can and will do it.
- The size of your success is determined by the size of your belief. So, think big goals and win big success.

You need to build confidence and destroy your fear within. Most of the fear we have today is psychological. Worry, tension, embarrassment are all built up with negative imagination. Fear is a powerful force which in one way or another prevents people from getting what they want from life. It actually makes people sick, shortens life, creates uncertainty and lack of confidence.

These two steps would help cure fear and win confidence:

- Isolate your fear: Determine exactly what you are afraid of.
- Take action: There is always some kind of action for any kind of fear. Remember that hesitation only enlarges and magnifies the fear.

Take action promptly and be decisive as lack of self-confidence can be traced directly to a mis-managed memory.

Some differences between a small thinker and a big thinker are as follows:

Situation	Short-sighted	Visionary
GOALS	Set small goals	Sets high goals
VISION	Sees only short term	See's long term
MISTAKES	Magnifies minor error and turns them into big issues.	Ignore errors of little consequences.
FUTURE	Views future as limited	Sees future as very promising.
PROGRESS	Believes in retrenchment or at best status quo	Believes in expansion
COMPETITION	Competes with the average	Competes with the best
CONVERSATION	Talks negative about everything, friends, company and competition.	Talks positive About friends, company and competition
WORK	Looks for ways to avoid work.	Looks for more ways of doing work and helping others.

'Your beliefs become your thoughts, Your thoughts become your words, Your words become your actions, Your actions become your habits ….Your values become your destiny' - Gandhi

Change your Action Habit:

- Be a doer, someone who does things.
- Don't wait for things to be perfect, they never will be. Expect obstacles and difficulties in the future and solve them as they are.
- Ideas alone won't bring success. They have value only when you act upon them.
- Use action to cure fear and gain confidence. Do what you fear, and see it disappear.
- Think in terms of now, such as you should say "I am starting right now." Tomorrow, next week, later and other similar words are often related to failure.
- Seize the initiative, show the ability and ambition to do.

The difference between success and failure is found in one's attitude towards setbacks, discouragement and other disappointing situations.

A few points that would help you to turn defeat into victory.

- Study setbacks to pave your way to success. When you lose, learn and then go on to win next time.
- Have the courage to give yourself constructive criticism. Seek out your faults and weakness and then correct them.
- Don't blame anyone, find out what went wrong. Remember blaming would not get you anywhere.
- Blend persistence with experimentation. Don't defocus and change your goals but try new approaches to achieve them.

Use goals to help you grow. A goal is an objective, a purpose, its more than a dream. It's a dream on which action is going to be taken. Goals are as essential to success as air is to life.

The most important thing we need to ask ourselves before we start this networking business is where do we want to go. You can break it up into work/home/social network.

You can ask:

- What level of income do I want?
- What kind of standard of living do I want to provide my family and myself?
- What kind of house do I want to live in?
- What kind of vacations do I want to take?
- What finances would be required to send my children abroad for higher education?
- What social groups do I want to join?

Retention

You don't drown by falling in water, you drown only if you stay there.

The biggest challenge you will face in network marketing business is retention. Yes, you need to tell the prospect, all the positives of the business but you also have to share the negative experiences which are inevitable in this business.

Most new people drop out of the business because their sponsor and upline told them about the good benefits, in other words the positive side, but they never told them regarding the negative aspects, or we can say the basic realities that everyone in this business must face.

As a result, people who are new to this business are not prepared for bad things that they will inevitably have to deal with- that is disappointment, rejections or people not turning up for meetings.

The key to improving retention rates starts with self- awareness and the first thing we need to be aware of is that this happens to everyone. Therefore, you can't change certain realities, but you can surely change how you respond to those realities. You need to understand that network marketing business isn't just about products or opportunities, it's about emotional relationships.

People buy in the business on an emotional high and buy out on an emotional low.

What the new people who leave this business fail to realize is that everyone has a feeling of negative emotions from time to time. Successful people are not immune to negative feelings, but they have learned to manage their feelings rather than letting their feelings manage them.

The most common negative feelings people experience in this networking business is disappointment, anger and depression.

Disappointment: The root cause of this problem is unrealistic expectations of ourselves and others. When you expect others to always behave in a way that benefits you then you're setting yourself up for disappointment. By thinking that people should work hard like I do, or they should have returned my call this way, you are surrounding yourself with negative thoughts leading to disappointment.

At times you say to yourself if I could be at a higher level in the success ladder, then you are measuring yourself against an expectation instead you should measure yourself by your actions and not your results.

- **Anger:** Everybody in this business gets frustrated from time to time by hearing "no" many times. The best way to deal with your anger is to protest it. If you let your anger, get inside of you it will lead to depression. Therefore, it's important to let your anger out.
- **Depression:** Most depression is situational. It is characterized by lack of energy, excitement, passion, focus and sleep. Situational depression can be resolved by either protesting, exercising or talking with a coach or therapist.

In other words, you have to go through your feelings to be done with them, talk about them and protest it if you want to put them behind you.

You need to actually get rid of your negative feelings in short by:

- Feeling it
- Expressing it
- Releasing it

Selling

Who's a salesperson?

Anyone who sells a product, service or an idea. Aren't we all selling?

A candidate at a job interview is selling his ability and the interviewer is selling his company.

A boy proposing to a girl.

Politician's giving speech to get votes. A husband and wife.

Our overall personality either leaves a favorable or an unfavorable impression on others. Everyone in every company is constantly selling either for or against the company.

Why do you think selling has become a bigger challenge today?

- The buyer has too many options.
- Competition has become sophisticated.
- Media has made people more knowledgeable and aware.

Competition is good as people have choices and can compare you with others. Success in selling really demonstrates survival of the fittest.

Every profession needs specialization. An architect cannot perform a brain surgery. A medical doctor cannot represent you in a lawsuit. A lawyer cannot construct a building.

The demand for good sales professionals is high but we don't have an education program for it.

Learning to sell is like learning to ride a bicycle. Remember, the first time when we were learning to ride a bicycle, we had three wheels to balance. First time we were scared and afraid that we might fall down but our objective was to eventually learn how to ride a bicycle without the third wheel while balancing. Just analyze this learning process. It was persistency and practice that brought proficiency. The exact same thing is true in learning to sell. Just like you cannot learn how to swim by reading a book similarly selling cannot be learnt or taught unless its practiced in reality.

Remember the world only rewards RESULTS and not efforts.

Selling is more a matter of will than skill and we need both. Will is more important than skill as skill can be matched but when you're feeling low that's the time your will is going to pull you up and that's what we call the winning edge.

If you see, the difference between ordinary and extra ordinary is "Extra."

Selling with integrity is a noble thing in this profession. At times you see negative perceptions develop towards certain professions based on the behavior of some individuals. Many people think that a salesperson is very fast and would sell his soul to make quick money, but they are only interested in their commissions/ bonus at any cost. We hear many times that to succeed you need to learn tricks of this trade but only cheats and crooks would learn these tricks. An honest person who's looking for a long-term relationship would only like to learn the trade.

People buy on emotions. For example, if you were offered a product which is identical in price and other terms and conditions, by two different companies who would you buy from? The answer is you will buy from the salesperson with whom you have a comfort level as people buy from their heart.

Therefore, as a salesperson we not only make a good presentation, but we sell ourselves first then the products and then the company.

Salesperson's actions are driven by positive values and attitudes which are intangible or invisible:

- Gratification
- Satisfaction
- Fulfillment
- Peace of mind

- Happiness
- Security
- Confidence

The tangible or visible rewards are:

- Monetary rewards (wealth)
- Recognition
- Respect
- Prestige
- Good life
- Comfort

Selling is transfer of enthusiasm from the seller to the buyer. It means you need to be confident of the product you're selling. You need to have complete knowledge about the product including its benefits. Therefore, selling is 90% conviction and 10% communication of the conviction.

Success is not measured by how we do as compared to others but how we do as compared to what we are capable of doing. It means you must compete against yourself to succeed.

So, what does a good sales professional have? He / she has a balance of character and competence both merged.

So, what is required to be a great salesperson?

- Commitment
- Focus on goals
- Acquiring competencies in selling skills
- Creating and following a selling system
- Putting in an organized effort
- Giving and taking respect
- Lead generation and prospecting

- Qualifying prospects
- Learning how to build rapport
- Building trust
- Identifying the decision-making process and key decision makers
- Fact finding and making presentation
- Learning to ask open ended questions
- Providing solutions
- Overcoming resistance / objections
- Closing a sale
- Finding the need of a customer
- Maintaining relationships after sale
- Avoiding mistakes and learning from experience
- Keeping yourself motivated and learning how to handle rejections

All the above points can be divided into 3 parts: pre-sale, during sale (actual sale) and post-sale.

The most important aspect of success is to have a positive attitude. Remember:

"Ability teaches us How to do our task,

Motivation decides Why we do it, and

Attitude determines How well we do it."

If we have a close look, some of the best salespeople don't have an advantage of higher education or a charming personality nor does a person needs to be aggressive in this field. What really separates a good salesperson from a mediocre is his attitude towards positivity, balance of mind, his ambitions which means focusing on goals with burning desire and his action which means implementing with a plan, which leads to translating your dreams into reality.

Every person has a different style of selling. It means there is uniqueness in every person. If you look deeply in about successful salespeople, you will notice that they are all positive thinkers. They feed their minds with positive thoughts daily. Now the question is what successful people do, and unsuccessful people don't. Well, you will be surprised to know that whether people successful or not don't like to work hard, but successful people do it anyways.

Successful people don't like to get up early in the morning nor do unsuccessful like to, but successful people do get up in the morning and follow their daily routine.

Successful people are disciplined, doing what needs to be done whether they feel like doing it or not. It is the spirit that strengthens our inner thoughts and reminds us of our dreams and goals. It gives us courage to do our best.

Our best might not be good enough for our success but that's why we need to do "self-realization" for continuous improvement.

Selling can be exciting and rewarding both financially and emotionally or it can be depressing and frustrating.

We always need to be positive whether we make a sale or not .It is a continuous learning process.

The profession of selling is rooted in understanding the problem and providing the right solution through the act of empathizing and honest persuasion so that it results in a mutually profitable commercial transaction.

Its recommended that you associate with people of high moral character because positive people reinforce positivity.

Formula for Success:
- Commitment
- Be passionate
- Have belief in your product and company

- Your value should be integrity
- Be persistent, optimistic, positive thinker and work hard as there is no substitute for it.
- Have complete knowledge about your company and products and about industry (competition).
- Keep learning through new educational programs.
- Self-realization after every meeting is important for continuous improvement.
- Be enthusiastic and empathize with your prospect (I feel, felt and found)
- Don't procrastinate. Don't be an escapist.
- Take pride in your work. Don't do it half-heartedly.
- Stand by your principles of integrity.

Edison said that " Success is 95% perspiration and 5% inspiration". What are the qualities that a successful salesperson need to have?

- Character – Doing things ethically
- Courage – Continue positively even with obstacles around
- Conviction – Belief in product of the company
- Clarity- Goals set with deadlines
- Competence – You have the will to do it and the skills to perform
- Communication – Effective Communication
  - Good Listening Skills
  - Positive Body Language

A good leader/networker/salesperson must ensure the following:

- Bringing new customers every week or month
- Retaining existing customers / consultants
- Generating new business from existing customers / consultants /distributors/associates etc.

- Establishing trust relationships
- Helping customers, consultants, distributors, associates to become more productive
- Providing good after sales service
- Building credibility and goodwill

Below Average Salespeople	Average Salespeople	Exceptional Salespeople
Money drives these people	Company driven	Goodwill and customer driven
Selfish	Self interest	Mutual interest
Don't do the right things	Does the right thing for wrong reason	Does the right thing for the right reason
Does little but has a big ego	Takes full credit for success	Takes credit and gives credit to those behind the scenes
	Tries to be only on the right side of the law.	Does work ethically
	Prestige driven	Performance driven
	Wants to make sale	Wants to make customers

Continuous education or improvement programs help in developing skills.

For example, a wood cutter worked in a company for almost 3 years but never got a raise. The company hired a new person and within a short span of time that person got a raise.

The old person who had been working for the past 3 years went to the supervisor and said, "I have been here for the last 3 years and never got any raise but this new person who recently joined got a raise".

The supervisor said that we are a result-oriented company. His output went up and he got a raise. The person went back and started working harder by putting in long hours, but his output didn't go up, so he went up to the new person and asked him "how did your output go up?" The person said that "after cutting every tree I take a break for 2 minutes to sharpen my axe, when did you sharpen your axe the last time?" The old person said, "3 years ago".

The moral of the story is that you need to sharpen your axe (skills) with continuous education.

Warm Personality:

As a salesperson, you are the face of the company and remember first impression is very important as we won't get another chance.

You must have a pleasing personality which means a positive attitude, good behavior, good dressing sense, etiquettes, manners etc. for starting to build a rapport with your prospect.

In sales, rejections take place many times. Remember that success is not measured by how high we go up in life but how many times we get up and start again after falling down.

Here one needs to remember that even the best salesperson faces rejection. He/she cannot sell 100%.

In sales, one should not take rejections personally, if you take it personally then you become demotivated and cannot prepare for the next meeting properly as your mind would be stressed.

Fear of failure creates negative emotions like fear, jealousy and anger which drains our energy. This fear is worse than failure itself. It leads to more failures because with every downfall our self-esteem goes down and the salesperson starts to blame everyone, the company, product, prospects etc.

Negative people are driven and controlled by fear. A good salesperson is confident and persistent.

Sales can be:
- B2B – Business to Business
- B2C – Business to Consumer

Direct or Indirect selling:

Direct selling is all about relationship building in relationship selling. Sincerity is the backbone. Relationship selling means long term commitment, having common goals, mutual respect, ongoing trust and cooperation.

Relationship selling means:

- People buy people first
- Then they buy from the people
- Then they buy from the company

Building a relationship is a process which requires behavior, events, activities or actions.

For example, have you been to a restaurant which has great food, but you find the waiter to be rude and the service is poor. Do you think you would go back to that restaurant? The answer is "No."

Everyone needs to go through a process. Just like an athlete does not get a gold medal just like that, he earns it by going through trainings and hard work.

Relationship selling is long term as compared to transactional selling which is short term.

Relationship selling is based on:

- Integrity
- Sincerity
- People
- Principle
- Values
- Soft sell
- Gain plus Retain

Our objective is to gain and retain customers. To gain we must convert transaction with relationship and customer satisfaction with loyalty.

We should never let a customer forget us, that means we must keep in touch with him/her regularly and not take them for granted. Keep in mind that he is being solicitated by your competitors as well. Remember it costs 4 to 5 times more to gain a new customer than to retain an existing one.

How do I identify leaders ?

You have to identify potential people with passion, coach them to become leaders and make them successful!!

That's the magic; leaders make your life easy and make you financially secure. If you ask a networker, they might say, "Yes, I have a few good leaders," but that's a common misconception. The truth is, great people aren't always leaders, they're simply great people.

A leader is much more than a good worker, a good recruiter. A network marketing leader is somebody who:

- Gets most out of the new distributors and helps them become more than they can become alone
- Will make sure his or her distributors order products every month
- Never complains to downline distributors/consultants
- Never complains or whines to the upline or the company
- Has his or her goals and aspirations
- Conducts regular opportunity meetings for you when you are away
- Makes sure: product display set up and meeting starts on time
- It is in personal control of their attitude and doesn't let outside influences control their success
- Sets strong personal example of steady focus on the ultimate goal

You are very fortunate financially if you have one real leader. Leaders are rare, they are how you measure your success in networking.

In case there is a disaster like:

- Press releasing unfair reports on your business, you would lose uncommitted leaders
- Temporary product shortage occurs, distributors would just leave

- If company adjusts a few policies and procedures, a few more distributors would exit because they fear change in their lives.

However, none of these disasters would affect your leaders. Your leaders would continue to recruit, build and motivate their downlines.

How to build your Network?

The most important thing you need to remember for success in network marketing business is to: "To build leaders and make them successful."

Here we are talking about leaders, which are 'RARE' and not about people being good. You might think what I am talking about but yes, I am talking about leaders, you might have good people within your network but that really doesn't mean that they are leaders.

A leader is much more than a good worker, recruiter and a network builder/ acoach.

We can summarize a good leader as:

- A person who gets most out of the people in his network by helping and guiding them through.
- A person who ensures that their network distributors place orders every month or on alternate months.
- A person who does not complain to downline distributors, nor do they talk negative about the company or their upline.
- A person who has short term and long-term goals and aspirations.
- A person who ensures regular opportunity meetings whether the upline leader is there or not. This person takes care of all essential chores required for the meeting (hall booking, catalogues, product display, presentation, sales tools etc.) Conducts the meeting in a professional manner with positive attitude.
- A person who sets a strong personal example by being focused on ultimate goal, doesn't allow outside influences control his success.

A person who has all the above qualities is a true leader, whom we are looking for to build our network successfully. Leaders who are determined know how to measure success in network marketing.

Distributors come and go. They don't have 100% commitment to their network marketing business. They think let me try this company for a while and then if the payout cheque is small, they quit.

Distributors have actually learned how to quit, quite easily. Since people come and go, you can't build your network on just distributors, you actually need leaders.

Distributor's actually start becoming doubtful on the company when the following things happen:

- If there is a temporary product shortage.
- If the company adjusts a few policies and procedures, they fear the change may impact them.

However, none of the above will affect your leaders. Your leaders will continue to build, recruit and motivate their downlines.

We have seen that there are many times when a networker approaches a company or distributor as his/her existing company has closed down or something happened in that organization. The networker approaches stating that they are looking for a sponsor and from their previous company which has closed down they have a network of more than 30,000 and now they are looking for support from a company and sponsor. Imagine at that time how the sponsor would feel, he or she would start dreaming that now I can retire, I am going to be rich etc.

Now that the networker (leader so called) joined but the sponsor didn't realize that the networker's group didn't have loyalty to this networker. Out of 30,000 group around 20,000 decided to retire from networking. They just didn't want to do anything. Now out of the 10,000 around 8000 didn't even know the leader and out of the balance of around 1500 they didn't like the leader and from the remaining 500 around 450 were not sure whether they wanted to join or not and that's left with 50 people who signed up slowly at their own pace. So out of 30,000 only 50 joined approximately and this is the reality.

Many new distributors see leaders doing well at other competitive network marketing company and they think maybe if I make this leader an offer, I might be able to steal him from his upline. He or she would quit from their present company and join the new distributors network (who gave the offer) at the new company.

What we actually need to do is find someone who is not a leader, someone who is dedicated and wants to learn this business. You need to ask this potential leader, if your sincere and you really want to do this business, I am going to work with you, teach you what you need to know to become a leader and continue until we build you a solid group and a full-time source of income.

Imagine you spend six months developing this person to be successful, we assure you that this newly developed leader would think highly of you and your commitment to his success.

After a few months or even a year, someone might try to approach your new leader with an offer to join their network. In that moment, your leader would likely respond by saying, "I can't be successful by constantly jumping between different network marketing opportunities. I know my immediate upline/sponsor has invested six months in helping me succeed, and I owe them my loyalty. Plus, I trust that my sponsor will continue working with me." This security comes from the strong relationships you've built with the leaders in your network. This is how you're consistently building your business with solid foundation for long-term success.

In network marketing we actually need to ensure real duplications take place. Real duplication means working together for at least six months at every available opportunity. It would mean travelling together for business development, presentations, trainings, meetings, motivational talks, opportunity meeting, prospecting etc. You will not believe it, but the outcome of the new leader would be more attractive, what I mean is they would know everything, what their upline/sponsor knew along with their own personal experience and wisdom. He/she would be the product of their upline's/sponsor's knowledge and their own unique personal understanding. He/she would be a better leader than their upline/sponsor.

When you spend that kind of time with someone and train them well guess what, they start duplicating immediately, mentoring their first potential leader. So, this person after six months would know more than his/her uplines.

Sorting for Potential leaders

Helping someone to become a leader requires a lot of work and time. We can't afford to spend six months with a pseudo leader. We need to be 100% sure that this potential leader prospect is serious. In any business, time is a valuable asset.

We need to check out this potential leader prospects commitment and sincerity. We need to ask this potential leader prospect; How do you feel about this business? And then listen.

There are a few types of commitment:

- The first commitment is when prospect says "Well I'll try" which means his commitment is weak.
- Second commitment is they might say "I will do the best I can."
- This commitment is better than the first as many distributors say something like this.
- The third commitment is when the prospect potential leader promises " I will do whatever it takes." We actually need this type of commitment.

1. When your potential prospect says they will try what does it mean? Does it mean if they don't get a bonus or commission cheque they would quit, or does it mean they will work for a few weeks and see if they want to continue or give up.

   You actually need to get a proper commitment when you talk like this, the prospect potential leader would say something like 'Are you telling me I actually have to go to the opportunity meetings, but I know how they end.' Do I need to use the products? Why can't I just sell?

   Some prospect potential leaders might say 'Why do I have to go to do trainings?' I want to be rich. Isn't there a shortcut? This is a distributor with no commitment and therefore can't be our potential leader.

2. Better Commitment: Now some potential prospect would say I want to be a leader, and you have my commitment that I'll do my best. Now this potential prospect would do their very best but if their best isn't good enough to make it to the top to become a leader, what do you think will happen? The potential prospect would say well I did my best, it just didn't work out.

    You really don't want to hear this after investing six months in your potential leader. This person gave their best efforts, worked hard but that didn't make them a leader. In this scenario we can say that this person is a really good distributor. We all love good, committed distributors but commitment level of "I will do my best is not good enough for you to risk your six months of day-to-day mentoring.'

3. When a potential prospect says 'I will do whatever it takes to become a leader, a person like this can handle any obstacles in their path to success, it may be rejection from friends, relatives or negativity around. This potential prospect would respond to challenges. It actually takes one leader to make you financially fortunate and imagine if you have two or three then you are rich.

Leaders are rare and we actually need to find the right potential prospect or distributor with proper commitment.

The way to multiply our efforts is to create leaders who can take care of their own groups/network. Duplicating ourselves by creating new leaders is the only way to build a large, massive network.

The first thing we need to do is define the difference between a distributor and a network marketing leader.

Distributors:

Distributors are not too serious; they come and go. Sometimes they work hard and build groups. Distributors are actually looking at the following points from network marketing business:

- Ability to save on personal purchase
- A chance to make retail sales and profits
- Personality Development
- Being around positive people
- Part time income for car/home EMI's or child's education
- Family holidays
- Rewards and Recognition

We need to support and serve our distributors to reach these goals, but the support should take 10% to 20% of our time because distributors don't need a lot of support. They don't want calls on trainings or opportunity meetings.

They want a call when the company head comes, or the company launches a new product. Let's not forget distributors are not fully committed.

It's really important to look for leaders because just imagine what you would like to have, One Leader or 100 distributors. Definitely One Leader! Why?

We need to understand that we will have to replace distributors as time goes on, instead of building this residual income that we are talking about we end up with a full-time job of replacing distributors.

We actually need to change our focus on leaders because that would change how we build our business. No doubt this person is not easy and not the fastest route to reach your goal, but this has proven to be the most successful way to build your business.

"To be successful in network marketing all you have to do is build leaders and make them successful."

What to teach leaders?

Now first thing we need to see is what leaders know that distributors don't know.

A good distributor would know the following:
- All about the products/company
- How to create rapport with prospects and be loyal
- How to be positive
- How to sponsor effectively
- How to duplicate

Remember if you are focusing on developing leaders your activities, viewpoints on situations would be different than any other networkers.

You might feel skeptical on the above if developing one leader versus 100 distributors. For this I would like to share with you an example of the Army where an Army General makes a lot of difference.

For example, imagine you have a battalion of 50,000 soldiers and 5 Generals. The enemy comes and attacks where the soldiers were resting, so next morning you'll see that there are only 5 Generals left, so with the five Generals can we rebuild the army? Yes, of course. The Generals are your leaders. Now imagine the opposite example where the enemy kidnaps the 5 Generals so in that case we are left with 50,000 soldiers but no leadership or direction. So, as you see, Generals are everything therefore leaders are important.

We need to plan on how to get leaders. So, the steps are as follows:
- Who is a leader? What is leadership?
- Where do we find leaders?

What is a leader?
- Someone who is always ready to learn and encourages others
- Someone who doesn't have unfinished work may it be anything

- Someone who is coachable and good with people (effective communicator)
- Someone who has a goal and is committed to succeed with proper action plan
- Someone with a vision, ready to overcome obstacles in their path to success
- Someone who knows how to handle day-to-day problems. Not allowing problems to move further down in the network and being problem solver.

How do I find leaders?

There are two ways to find leaders:

- Stealing them from other networks by giving them an extra amount or supporting them in other ways. The only issue is if we steal leaders, that means they are temporary, and we would have to keep replacing them every now and then. They are not going to give you permanent income. These so-called leaders can move to any network if someone else offers them a better deal.
- Building leaders, from basics or scratch. We need to find a good potential distributor who's not a leader at present. We would have to hand hold this person and teach them exactly how to become a leader.

Now come across many people who would say they want to become a leader but it's not possible to train everyone who makes this statement because we need to see how committed they are; therefore, you need to give them a task to see their commitment. "Don't believe what people say, only observe what they do."

Give them a book to read and tell them that you will connect with them after three days to discuss the book. If this person is serious and committed, he would be enthusiastic on reading the book immediately and instead of waiting for three days that person would call you the next morning and start discussing the highlights of the book in details and ask any questions they have. Now this person is all set to learn to become a leader. Action speaks louder than words!

We would come across those people also who would say "Oh was too busy. Didn't get time to read after three days also." By doing this test of giving books/CD's/videos etc. it would help us not to waste time on those who are actually not committed or serious.

Committed.

But knowing the above things doesn't make this person a leader. The only difference between leaders and distributors is the "way they think." Yes, how they think!

In every situation or problem, a leader will think differently than a distributor. So, if we train our distributors to think differently when problems, challenges or situations arise then we will have better trained leader.

How can we teach?

Well, we would make a list with problems, challenges and some situations that might arise, then teach them how and what to think.

For example, you have taken an order along with the amount for the product and then you place this order, and you come to know it's a back order! Now in a situation like this a distributor's thought process you would say that customer needed the order. He/she is my friend's colleague, what is he/she going to think about me and my service. He/she had given me money immediately for that order and my reputation will be ruined. What are my friends going to think, my company can't even keep products in stock? If they can't keep products in stock, they might not be able to pay commission or bonus, this way things can't work out, it's terrible, I quit!

Everyone has problems whether it's a leader or a distributor but it's our attitude and thought process which makes a leader think on how to handle problems and challenging situations.

Now in the above-mentioned back-order situation, a leader would say these products are so much in demand that even if my customers give me money, they still can't get the products. Its selling so well that even the company can't keep products in stock. My new customers would be happy to know that the product is so good, and he/she would probably order two or three times more products to make sure he/she can get some. It means more sales and more commission/bonus.

Another common problem we hear in network marketing is that my sponsor doesn't help me because of which I haven't been able to recruit anyone. My sponsor doesn't know more about this business than I do. This is distributor thinking than leadership thinking. Reality is that this sponsor has recruited other people, maybe out of many that this sponsor recruited only two or three became successful and the question is how they became successful.

Another common problem we hear is my sponsor lives too far away. I can't become successful because my sponsor doesn't come to help me. We actually need to shift our thinking to leadership thinking by giving the below example. Imagine you're taking a flight to Mumbai and there is another passenger sitting next to you in the flight. You start having casual conversation.

You – Hi! How are you?

My name is XYZ. Passenger – Fine thanks.

My name is ABC. Passenger – Fine thanks.

You– Where are you working?

Passenger – I am President of a club which has more than 10,000 members. We have regular jobs, but we meet in evening's. Most of my friends are interested in networking but we haven't come across a company that we would love to join, which has a good marketing plan, good products etc.

You – You're thinking that your business opportunity is going to be great for this person.

You – Where do you live?

Passenger – Bengaluru

You – Your first thought as a distributor, Oh how can I sponsor this person as I would only be able to support him locally, but now you start thinking like a leader and you say: I am working with a great network marketing company, who has good quality products and attractive business opportunity.

Passenger – Great so when can I join? How would you support me as I live in Bengaluru?

You – It doesn't make a difference because when we join network marketing we are provided with an opportunity, not an entitlement. It's up to us to take advantage of the opportunity. Our success in network marketing is up to us not our sponsor. In fact, we choose to be successful, even if our sponsor did not exist. In network marketing business as a sponsor, you can recruit anyone anywhere, you cannot make this statement that I can't be successful because I don't have a local sponsor to help me, nor can you keep shifting your house every time you recruit someone outside your locality.

Another common thing we hear very often is products are too expensive, no one wants to pay that much, now this is distributor thinking. A leader would say people buy for convenience, quality, comfort, extra features or prestige. Most people will pay more for products when they can get this extra convenience quality, comfort, extra features or prestige.

A leader needs to give examples through stories to change the thought process of a potential distributor to become a leader. Such as:

Distributor – People buy because of the price.

Leader – Lets go outside and stand on the road. Now tell me what's the cheapest car you can purchase.

Distributor – Tata Nano. That's the least expensive car you can get. It has four wheels, and it would get you from point A to point B.

Leader – Let's see how many people on this road are driving this least expensive car. I think it would be more than 50% of the cars that will pass by us which will be Tata Sumo.

Now when we will stand and see what types of automobiles pass by us. Well, we see Honda, Audi, Ford, Maruti, Hyundai and Volkswagen. We don't see Tata Nano.

Leader – Lets go down to another road, what do we see here again? Chevrolet, Toyota, Ford, Honda etc.

Distributor – It doesn't look like anybody purchases cars based on price. They actually purchase comfort, color, convenience, image, special features, speed and prestige. You have changed my thought process.

It's important that as a leader that we explain with proper story examples, so that we can change the distributors thought process.

Just think of all possibilities of proving to your distributor that people don't buy on lowest price.

You can stand outside an expensive shoe store and watch the people's purchase.

People pay a good amount of money to go to concerts just to listen to their favorable music.

Sometimes people order pizza from outside instead of making it at home, which would be more cost effective, because of taste, convenience and comfort. So, people don't buy on lowest price.

You will come across distributors who want to become a leader, but they are not willing to invest in companies support materials (products, sales aids, training material etc.)

They say they have no money but when you ask them, "Do you go out for dinner? they say "yes," "Do you smoke?" they say "yes", "Do you drink?" they say "yes" and "Do you party?" they say "yes".

They have money for all the above things, but they feel they should not waste money on materials which would help them in many ways to achieve success. People like this come and tell you nothing has worked so far for me so how can I continue like this Mr. Sponsor.

The point I want to make here is that it's not about money, it's about priorities. If this potential prospect or distributor fails to perceive enough value in your opportunity, they will never have money for support material. The solution is we create the value of our opportunity in our distributors mind or make a choice of investing time with this distributor to teach him/her to become a leader. If we actually look at all the networking leaders, some leaders have successful upline sponsors and some were sponsored by unsuccessful distributors/leaders. We can say that most upline sponsors have successful distributors and unsuccessful distributors. Now the question is that if both successful and unsuccessful distributors have the same sponsor then the only variable is the distributor.

Building leaders is easy once you teach them how to handle problems. Networkers everywhere are killing their own business by getting involved in everyday small problems. The stress they take both mental and physical, and amount of time it takes up is absolutely ridiculous.

In summary unsuccessful leaders quickly get into the fix it mode and spend their most valuable time making sure nothing bad happens to anyone in their downline, upline or company. Whereas successful leaders don't waste their time trying to change people, they sort out their perceived problems or try to eliminate all the problems. They learn to manage problems and not fix them. Successful leaders come to agreement with the fact that problems would be there every now and then, we just need to live with it and not take stress.

All network marketing companies have problems, problems will come and go, a few might stay on, but we need to concentrate on developing leaders as once we actually develop these leaders they will stay on, which means loyalty, longterm regular income / earnings.

The most important thing we need to teach our distributors or anyone joining our network is that they need to decide if the problem is larger than their dreams for success or their dreams for success is larger than the problem.

Let's list down certain problems we actually hear about in network marketing business.

- The Products are expensive
- Retail Profit is less
- Compensation plan pays too little, not competitive
- Courier charges for shipping orders is high
- Order not delivered on time
- My name is not there in the Newsletter or Achievers list
- My commission /bonus is not calculated correctly
- There are a few mistakes in my Genealogy report
- No good videos to show prospects
- No one making money
- Sales is low and there are no recruitment
- Out of stock problem
- Sales volume requirements are high for incentives
- Company doesn't offer many trainings
- Company keeps making changes every now and then
- No one wants to join
- My spouse and children don't listen to me
- It's difficult to place an online order, it should be simplified
- My credit note for my products returned is still not reflecting in my e-wallet.
- My sponsor doesn't help

- Back-order issues
- Discontinuation of your downlines favorite products.

Now despite all the above problems many leaders are still successful. Therefore, it's important we prepare not only ourselves but also our downlines /network in advance for problems. Difficulties would be there in all walks of life cause that's 'LIFE.'

No Company is perfect, we as humans are bound to make mistakes.

Now after listening to above if the distributor is ready to give 100% commitment, then it's great.

It's not necessary that this advance conversation works all the time but it's a good start to preparing them.

www.ingramcontent.com/pod-product-compliance
Lightning Source LLC
LaVergne TN
LVHW061600070526
838199LV00077B/7126